WOMEN AND WAR

THE WOMEN BEHIND ROSIE RIVETER

Working for the U.S. War Effort

by Pamela Dell

CAPSTONE PRESS
a capstone imprint

Snap Books are published by Capstone Press,
1710 Roe Crest Drive, North Mankato, Minnesota 56003
www.mycapstone.com

Library of Congress Cataloging-in-Publication Data
Names: Dell, Pamela, author.
Title: The women behind Rosie the Riveter : working for the U.S. war effort /by Pamela Dell.
Other titles: Working for the U.S. war effort Description: North Mankato, Minnesota : Snap Books, Capstone Press,
[2018] | Series: Women and war | Includes bibliographical references and index. |Audience: Grades 4-6. | Audience:
Ages 8–14.Identifiers: LCCN 2017015340| ISBN 9781515779353 (library binding) |
ISBN 9781515779438 (pbk.) | ISBN 9781515779476 (ebook pdf)
Subjects: LCSH: World War, 1939–1945—Women—United States. | World War, 1939–1945—War work—United States. |
Rosie the Riveter (Symbolic character) | Rosie, the riveter. | Parker-Fraley, Naomi, 1924– |
Doyle, Geraldine Hoff, 1924–2010. | Women—Employment—United States—History—20th century. |
Women—United States—Biography.
Classification: LCC D810.W7 R577 2012 | DDC 940.53082092/273—dc23

LC record available at https://lccn.loc.gov/2017015340

Editorial Credits
Megan Atwood, editor; Veronica Scott, designer; Jo Miller, media researcher

Image Credits
Alamy: Sheldon Levis, 27 (top), Terry Smith Images, 14; AP Images, 24, The State Journal, Robert Killips, 21;
Getty Images: Bettmann, 8, 11, 19, 23, Buyenlarge, 25, New York Daily News Archive, 15, San Jose Mercury News, 27
(bottom); Library of Congress, 4, 6; National Park Service, 13; Newscom: Everett Collection, 16; Shutterstock: Everett
Historical, 10, 12, KathyGold, cover, TinaImages, 26

Design Elements
Shutterstock: Allexxandar, Eky Studio, udra11

Printed and bound in the United States of America.
000757

TABLE OF CONTENTS

u think you can do a man's job, huh? A little
ou?" The factory boss looked Evie up and down,
ing his smirk. He puffed on his smelly cigar.

ie was not backing
at's right, sir."
ssed her arms and
oss her steadiest
as 1943, and the
ved and hoped to
off fighting World
39–1945). As soon
eard about war
obs opening up for
e'd bought a train
'd traveled all the
rural Virginia to
ork in Baltimore,
ready to do her
he wanted was to
fighter planes so
could win the war.

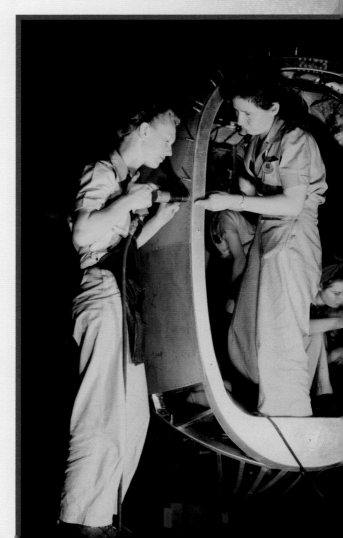

"How old are you, Evelyn?" the boss asked now.

"Twenty-four, sir," she replied, "and believe me, I can do this work — as good as any man!"

The boss burst out with a big laugh. But he stood up, stubbed out his cigar, and put his hands on his hips. "You know anything about riveting?"

"No. But I can do it if you train me," Evie said in her most confident voice. She knew they used big, heavy drill-like tools called riveting guns to put the plane parts together. The rivets were short metal bolts that shot out of the gun to join two pieces of metal. That was about all she knew. But it didn't matter — she was ready.

"Come on, then." The boss cocked his head and motioned Evie to follow him down to the big bay where the planes were being built. Most of the employees were women, since most of the men were fighting overseas. "We'll get you working on the tails of the planes and see how well you do."

"I'll do just fine," Evie assured the man. Her stomach was scrunching with nerves. But she had strong arms from bucking bales. She was a quick learner. And now she'd have a good job with a decent salary — something to really be proud of.

Another "Rosie" had joined the workforce.

5

Though the scenario on the previous pages is made up, it reflects the reality of the United States in the early 1940s. World War II had been raging in Europe since 1939. In December 1941 the United States entered the war too. With that a patriotic fever broke out overnight. Thousands of American men rushed to enlist. But many more — 10 million — were drafted.

Gearing up for war required massive effort. Factories went into full-production mode. Aircraft and tanks needed to be built. Guns, bombs and bullets had to be produced. Every soldier needed uniforms and equipment of all kinds.

This huge war effort would need millions of workers to replace the men who had left. Who would take their places and fill the new jobs being created?

I'm Proud... my husband _wants_ me to do my part
SEE YOUR U. S. EMPLOYMENT SERVICE
WAR MANPOWER COMMISSION

World War II U.S. poster

FACT

Although African-American women faced racism, they held jobs in every war industry. They worked at all levels, from the most to the least skilled. Women with college degrees, domestic workers in the homes of wealthy people, and field workers from rural southern communities all joined the war effort.

The answer was obvious. Women would have to fill these jobs. Most of the work would be in the defense industry. The government would need to recruit women for what was typically men's work. They would build ships and tanks and bombers. They would be working on assembly lines. They would labor at hard, grimy, and dangerous jobs. How would the U.S. government attract women to work like this?

The answer was advertising. The government mounted a widespread campaign to recruit women. It worked. One of this extended ad campaign's most successful symbols was a figure who became known as "Rosie the Riveter." Today "Rosie" is just as well known as she was 75 years ago — and her fame only continues to grow.

Women at Work

Before the war only one percent of aviation industry workers were women. By 1943 that number had increased to a whopping 65 percent, or 310,000 female workers. But women were needed everywhere. They met the call and rose to the challenge. In 1940 27 percent of American women worked outside the home. By 1945 another 10 percent had joined the workforce. Almost one quarter of all married women were now taking home a salary.

"These jobs will have to be glorified as a patriotic war service if American women are to be persuaded to take them and stick to them. Their importance to a nation engaged in total war must be convincingly presented."

— *from the Basic Program Plan for Womanpower Office of War Information*

America's entry into the war took effort from every industry. But the availability of more jobs was good news for Americans. The United States was just coming out of the Great Depression (1929–1939). The war and its opportunities for economic growth conclusively ended it. With these new jobs, incomes rose for almost everyone. Salaries for both skilled and unskilled laborers increased. And working women made more money too.

The auto industry stopped manufacturing cars to concentrate on building war machines.

LAST "GREAT" 1942 PLYMOUTH
Our tanks and guns
will be "GREAT" too!
THEN WE'LL BUILD AGAIN
MORE "GREAT CARS"
Plymouth Plant Employees

The Male-Female Pay Gap

Women were as necessary to the war effort as men. But they were paid much less. In 1944 skilled male workers averaged about $54.65 a week. Women with the same skills averaged only about $31.21 per week. Even today, nearly 75 years later, serious salary inequalities still exist. Women in the United States earn on average only 80 percent of what men are paid. The pay gap is even greater for women of color. And change is slow. Experts predict that men and women will not make equal salaries until 2152.

Aviation, shipbuilding, and armaments were big war industries. But things quickly changed for many companies that made consumer goods like cars. Now they were also pressed into service to help the war effort. The auto industry resisted at first. But by 1943 car makers had begun mainly building aircraft instead of automobiles.

By then all these industries were accepting women as employees. But they might not have found the numbers they needed if it hadn't been for Rosie the Riveter.

In August 1942 the government's War Manpower Commission (WMC) put together a team called the Women's Advisory Committee. Its main job was figuring out the best way to draw women into the workforce. The committee estimated that 5 million employees were needed in 1943, and most of them would have to be women.

Soon after, the WMC made its first efforts to recruit women. They hired New York City ad agencies. These experts designed many different kinds of ads to appeal to women. The ads played on the radio and at the movies. Billboards and posters also got the message across. The campaign urged women to take jobs in the name of patriotism. In late 1942 one ad came right out and said it: "Women Workers Will Win the War."

SOLDIERS *without guns*

World War II U.S. propaganda poster targeting women

The main target of these ads was middle-class married white women. Most of these women had never worked outside the home. At that time most working-class white women and working-class and middle-class African-Americans were already employed. Because this was normal during that era, those women were considered easier to recruit. But it was different for married middle- and upper-class white women. For them having to go to work was seen as a disgrace. This perception had to change. And the ad campaigns helped that happen.

FACT

One Baltimore ad used a comparison housewives could relate to. The ad pointed out that industrial jobs were "a lot more exciting than polishing the family furniture."

Almost all the ads showed the targeted "type" — white, married, and young. Ethnic diversity in these campaigns was rare. Once in a while an ad might be directed at "older" women. One such ad showed a woman holding a riveting tool. The caption read, "Grandma's got her gun." But even those "grandmas" weren't very old. In the Washington, D.C., war offices "older" was defined as women over 35.

All these efforts were successful from the start. But it was a fictional character that really sparked public imagination. That character was Rosie the Riveter. Through Rosie the idea of women going to work became a good thing. Women started to feel that war work wasn't just acceptable. It could even be desirable.

"The hand that rocks the cradle can also run a drill press."
— *slogan in WWII ad campaign*

FACT

Before the war, most working women had been young and single. Most had non-industrial "pink collar" jobs, often as secretaries, salesgirls, or teachers. But during the war, 72 percent of female employees were married women. And by the war's end in 1945, 50 percent of all working American women were older than 35.

WE CAN DO IT!

Before the war discrimination had been a major barrier for women who wanted to work. When they applied for jobs, they were usually passed over in favor of men. If they did get hired they often weren't treated fairly. For women of color gender discrimination and racism were both obstacles. Only rarely did any women earn equal wages.

The iconic poster that sparked a movement

But as the war-work ads continued women took notice. They applied for jobs, and got them. Taking over for millions of men helped them realize that they could do the same work and do it well. The seeds of equality began to take early root in armament factories, industrial plants, and shipyards. There, millions of "Rosies" found a new kind of freedom. Nothing would be the same again. The ads and posters had worked.

Today one of those posters is particularly familiar. It is also most often associated with the Rosie the Riveter character. But it didn't start out that way.

The iconic poster shows a young woman in a red bandanna. Her sleeve is rolled up to show off her bicep. Above her the big, bold caption reads, "We Can Do It!" The poster appeared in a Westinghouse Electric Company factory. Its purpose was to motivate wartime workers, men and women alike. And at the time it had nothing to do with anyone named Rosie or any other specific person.

Rather Rosie got her start as a song. That song titled "Rosie the Riveter" was written in 1942 by Redd Evans and John Jacob Loeb. The lyrics told of a patriotic girl "working overtime on the riveting machine." The catchy tune quickly caught on. It became the first step in Rosie's "career." She was definitely going places.

"All the day long, whether rain or shine
She's a part of the assembly line
She's making history, working for victory
Rosie the riveter!
Everyone stops to admire the scene
Rosie at work on the B-Nineteen
She's never twittery, nervous or jittery
Rosie the Riveter"

— "Rosie the Riveter" song lyrics

The idea of Rosie the Riveter as a "tough wartime cookie" was taking off. She'd gotten her start in a song. But soon after, she became a cover girl. In those years, the *Saturday Evening Post* was a well-established weekly magazine. It had a circulation of more than 4 million. The highly acclaimed illustrator Norman Rockwell often did covers for the *Post*. On May 29, 1943, the magazine published his latest.

The illustration showed a muscular working girl taking a lunch break. She was dressed in jeans and a work shirt. She had her goggles pushed up and a sandwich in one hand. In her lap sat a giant riveting gun. This picture captured the independent working girl of the war years. Rockwell had no doubt heard the popular Rosie song. He left a clue that proved it. The girl's name is printed on her lunchbox: Rosie.

Norman Rockwell's
Rosie the Riveter

Modeling for Rosie

Nineteen-year-old Mary Doyle Keefe wasn't expecting to be a model. She worked as a telephone operator in Arlington, Vermont, but when her nationally acclaimed neighbor Norman Rockwell made the offer, she was interested. Rockwell asked Mary if she would pose for a new painting he was doing. She agreed. That now-famous oil painting was Rockwell's *Rosie the Riveter.*

The pose that appeared on the magazine cover was the artist's second try. He had first asked Mary to wear a white shirt and saddle shoes. But then he changed his mind and had her wear a blue shirt and penny loafers. Mary really had held a ham sandwich. But the riveting gun was only a lightweight prop. And Rockwell felt he owed Mary an apology. She had a slight, 110-pound (50-kilogram) build. But the artist had made her look much huskier on canvas.

Rockwell paid Mary $10 for posing for him. In 2002 his painting sold at auction for $4.95 million. Today it has a permanent home. It hangs in the Crystal Bridges Museum of American Art in Bentonville, Arkansas.

"I'm proud of this painting. It's a symbol of what women did for the war, to do their part and to give up their nail polish."

— Mary Doyle Keefe, 1994

Chapter 4

CHANGE IN THE AIR

As the 1940s wore on, the concept of Rosie the Riveter gained popularity. Women flooded into — and were doing well at — jobs that had formerly been entirely "men's territory." They built Jeeps and tanks as well as airplanes. They operated drill presses, welding tools, and heavy, assembly-line machinery.

The efforts to get women on the job went beyond ads and posters. The cover photo of the August 9, 1943, issue of *Life* magazine showed a female steelworker at work in her goggles, cap, and heavy gloves. In 1944, a B-grade Hollywood romantic comedy titled *Rosie the Riveter* was released. In-store displays, promotional films, and magazine and newspaper articles also added to the call. Even museums got behind the campaign.

FACT

Riveters worked in pairs. One woman would shoot the rivets through the metal. The "bucker" would then use a bucking bar on the other side to press the rivets flat. These teams were often made up of one white woman and one woman of color.

Movie poster of
Rosie the Riveter

African-American women benefitted in one important way from this new push for female employees. In many cases the war-industry jobs gave them an escape from the Jim Crow laws of the South. These were laws that segregated blacks and whites in everything from schools to restaurants to public transportation. Now, in factories and other businesses across the country, black and white women worked side by side.

With this integration of the workforce came change. Women's outlook about what they could and could not do shifted. Now, their desire for equal rights and equal opportunities had been awakened. This new awareness led directly to even greater changes. Only a decade or so later, the Civil Rights movement would be born.

"You came out to California, put on your pants, and took your lunch pail to a man's job. This was the beginning of women's feeling that they could do something more."

— Sybil Lewis, a Lockheed Aircraft riveter

The United States has come a long way in job equality since World War II. But when the war ended in 1945, millions of dedicated, patriotic, working women got a big shock. Throughout the war they had worked long, hard hours in the defense industry. They had committed themselves to their jobs and their country. They had made sure the United States had what it needed to wage war. The women had gained confidence and independence. Plus their work had brought them regular paychecks.

The raw deal came when most of the Rosies were abruptly let go. As American men returned from war looking for work, women began getting a new message. Before they had been a critically necessary part of the workforce. Now they were suddenly being told to get back home where they belonged. For many women it was like a slap in the face. They hadn't thought of themselves as only temporary workers.

Some women were glad to resume a "normal" home life in a more traditional role. But for countless female riveters and other workers, losing their jobs was a bitter disappointment. These women had a hard time accepting this sudden change. They did not want to go back to a life of domestic chores, husbands who told them what to do, and no money of their own.

But despite this loss the image of Rosie — strong, skilled, and sure of herself — lived on. The women who had worked for the war effort had lost their jobs. But they could feel proud of what they had done.

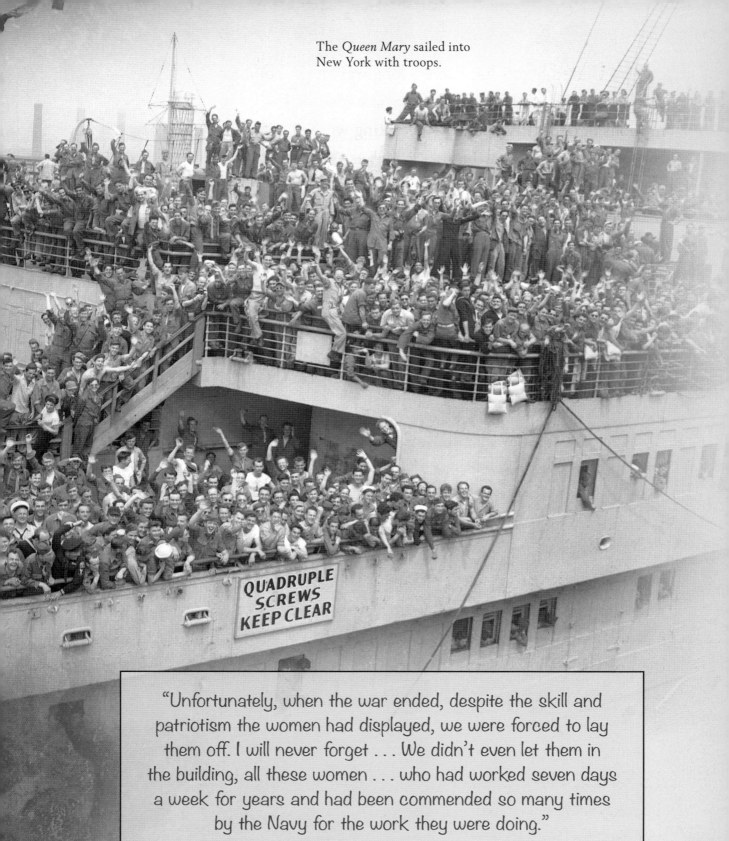

The *Queen Mary* sailed into New York with troops.

QUADRUPLE
SCREWS
KEEP CLEAR

"Unfortunately, when the war ended, despite the skill and patriotism the women had displayed, we were forced to lay them off. I will never forget . . . We didn't even let them in the building, all these women . . . who had worked seven days a week for years and had been commended so many times by the Navy for the work they were doing."

— *William Mulcahy, a wartime factory supervisor*

During the war years "Rosie the Riveter" hadn't yet been directly connected with the Westinghouse poster. And in the decades after the war the whole concept was all but forgotten. Then in 1982 Rosie got a revival. That year the *Washington Post* newspaper ran a story about old propaganda campaigns. Westinghouse's "We Can Do It!" poster appeared in the article. That image struck a chord with the evolving feminist movement.

Women related to the strong, confident, attractive girl with her raised fist and tough, determined expression. Women everywhere adopted the image. Their own struggles for equality made them appreciate the ideals and the spirit of the 1940s working women.

From then on J. Howard Miller's "We Can Do It!" girl became linked with Rosie the Riveter. In time it became a symbol of women's equality with men. But did the girl in the poster have a real-life counterpart? And if so, who was she?

FACT

Norman Rockwell's famous *Saturday Evening Post* illustration clearly identifies the figure as Rosie. But that image never became associated with Rosie the Riveter in the same widespread way the nameless "We Can Do It!" girl did. Why not? Simply because Rockwell owned the copyright to his illustration. He didn't allow his painting to be mass produced as the poster was.

There is no question who the "real" Rosie was in Rockwell's *Post* cover. But people wondered about the Westinghouse poster Rosie for decades. In the war years, many other Rosies were linked to Miller's bandanna-clad girl. But the one who got the most credit for the longest number of years was a woman named Geraldine Hoff Doyle.

Geraldine Hoff Doyle holds the iconic Rosie the Riveter image.

In 1984 60-year-old Geraldine picked up a copy of *Modern Maturity* magazine. Inside she got a blast from the past. An uncaptioned photo pictured a young woman in a polka dot bandanna. She was shown operating a big piece of metal machinery. Geraldine had worked briefly in a metal pressing factory. Now she saw herself in that photo. And the article linked the photo with Miller's "We Can Do It!" poster.

The rest was history — for a while. Convinced she was the girl in that picture, Geraldine notified the press. It was a big deal. The girl who inspired Miller's work had been found! Geraldine began making public appearances. Everyone associated her with the poster.

Then came a surprise. In 2009 85-year-old Naomi Parker Fraley went to a Rosie the Riveter reunion. It was held at the WWII Home Front National Historical Park in California. There she saw a display with a photograph she recognized. It was the same photo Geraldine had seen 25 years earlier. Along with the picture was a copy of the Miller poster.

The woman pictured in the display was identified as Geraldine. But it was actually Naomi. Naomi knew this for sure because she had a copy of that photo of herself. It had been taken in 1942 at the Alameda (California) Naval Air Station. She had worked there on a machine called a turret lathe, just as pictured.

FACT

In March 1942 Naomi's captioned photo appeared in big-city newspapers from Oakland to Milwaukee to Washington, D.C. "I even got fan mail!" Naomi Parker Fraley said.

Naomi tried to set the record straight with the parks department where the reunion was held. She sent them a news clipping with the photo. Its caption clearly named her. But so much time had passed it was impossible to change what the public already believed.

This case of mistaken identity didn't come to light until much later. In 2015 a New Jersey communications professor named James J. Kimball tracked Naomi down. He'd spent six years looking for her. Like many others, he believed J. Howard Miller's "We Can Do It!" girl had been inspired by that now familiar photo. Naomi showed the professor her proof of being the girl in that picture. It was a success both of them could finally enjoy.

Naomi Parker working at the Alameda Naval Air Station

"She had been robbed of her part of history. It's so hurtful to be misidentified like that . . . and there's nothing you can do because you're 95 and no one listens to your story."

— *James J. Kimble*

Chapter 6

ROSIE'S LEGACY

Today Rosie the Riveter is a pop culture icon. The poster image has taken on more and more power as a symbol of feminist pride and independence. Rosie signifies women's equality with men. And the real Rosies, so crucial to the 1940s war effort, have not been forgotten. They are being celebrated and acknowledged in many ways.

The biggest national tribute to Rosie can be found in Richmond, California. During World War II 56 different war-related industries were located in the town. This included four big shipyards. So it's fitting that Richmond's waterfront is now home to Rosie the Riveter/Home Front National Historical Park. The park honors the millions of women who worked for the war industry.

Rose Will Monroe was another "Rosie" who caught the public's eye.

Rosie the Riveter mural in Sacramento, California

The Rosie Trust also does important research. Among other projects, the trust collects women's wartime stories. It displays historical artifacts. All this reflects the working Rosies' past. The trust organizes benefit dinners, Rosie reunions, and in-school presentations. It regularly offers youth programs like Rosie's Girls, where young women learn practical Rosie-like job skills. They also gain the confidence to achieve their best.

There's also the American Rosie the Riveter Association. They post true Rosie stories, offer student educational grants, host Rosie conventions and reunions, and sell Rosie-related products.

All these programs are a dynamic and important part of the Rosie the Riveter legacy.

Rosie the Riveter is an image that seems to be popping up everywhere these days, with good reason. Young women today have reaped the benefits of the Rosies who went to work in tough jobs half a century ago. Most people now take for granted that women can be doctors, lawyers, mechanics, and machinists — anything they wish to be. The United States has come a long way in job equality since World War II. But women have not yet won the fight for complete equal rights.

A stamp from 1999

The "We Can Do It!" Rosie is like a visual rallying cry. She can be found in countless forms. In 1999, she got her own postage stamp. Since then her likeness has been printed on T-shirts, mugs, and lapel pins. There are Rosie action figures and Rosie tattoos. She appears on wall art. Countless books and movies center on Rosie stories, both fiction and nonfiction. People dress up as Rosie for Halloween and costume parties. The Rosie figure has also been recreated as many different women of color. In some versions she wears a hijab.

Celebrities have gotten into it too. Beyoncé has appeared as Rosie to show her feminist pride. Former First Lady Michelle Obama made her own version of the poster to promote the recovery.gov website.

The Rosie momentum is unlikely to die down. And that's understandable. In a way, the real-life Rosies cracked opened a door. Their labors during the war let in the earliest hints of equal rights for women. The door has now been cast wide open, and it won't be shut again. And that is the true legacy of Rosie the Riveter.

Vending machine in Pearl Harbor, Hawaii

Rosie's Widespread Influence

Rosie the Riveter has made a name for herself in sports and even in world records. The New York Riveters, a National Women's Hockey League team, have the familiar Rosie pose as their logo. The Rockford Riveters are a female tackle football team based in Rockford, Illinois. Detroit, Michigan, is home to a Rosie the Riveter drill team. And in 2016 2,229 people dressed as Rosie gathered at the Rosie the Riveter/World War II Home Front National Historical Park in Richmond, California. That crowd set the 2016 *Guinness Book of World Records* record for the largest number of Rosies gathered in one place.

ROSIE THE RIVETER

December 7, 1941

The Japanese bomb Pearl Harbor. The United States declares war on Japan the next day.

February 1942

Redd Evans and John Jacob Loeb release their iconic song "Rosie the Riveter."

March 1942

A photograph of a young woman working on a turret lathe at the Alameda, California, Naval Air Station appears in newspapers throughout the country.

August 1942

The War Manpower Commission (WMC) forms the Women's Advisory Committee to find ways to get women into the workplace.

February 1943

J. Howard Miller, a Pittsburgh artist, creates a poster with the caption "We Can Do it!" The girl in the poster is most likely inspired by the girl in the Naval Air Station photo. The poster is displayed for two weeks in a Pennsylvania factory. Eventually it becomes iconic as a depiction of "Rosie the Riveter."

May 29, 1943

Norman Rockwell's *Rosie the Riveter* painting appears on the cover of the *Saturday Evening Post*

June 1943

Due to huge reader interest, the *Post* follows up the "Rosie" issue with a long article about Rockwell and the symbolic meaning of his painting. In July *Art Digest* magazine does a similar analytical article. This second article leads to the painting going on tour.

August 9, 1943

Life magazine does a feature story called "The Many Faces of Rosie the Riveter" with a cover photo showing a female steelworker on the job.

September 1943

Magazines across the country respond to an earlier request by the Magazine War Guide. The guide asked that all U.S. magazines run a "women and work" cover in September as a joint effort to promote women joining the workforce.

TIMELINE

1944

Hollywood releases *Rosie the Riveter*, a romantic comedy about a female factory worker.

1945

Most of the 2 million women working in the war industry lose their jobs to veterans returning from the war.

1980

The documentary film *The Life and Times of Rosie the Riveter* is released. It includes interviews with 700 real-life Rosies and others involved in the propaganda effort.

1984

Geraldine Hoff Doyle mistakenly identifies herself as the "Rosie" in the Alameda Naval Air Station photograph. She gains widespread attention as the "real" Rosie the Riveter. Also the movie *Swing Shift* hits theaters. The story follows the lives of five female aircraft workers in the 1940s.

1999

The U.S. Postal Service issues its "Rosie the Riveter" postage stamp, which is a reproduction of the "We Can Do It!" poster. Also that year a toy manufacturer releases a Rosie the Riveter action figure. A joking marketing comment at the time was, "You can use her to beckon your Barbies out of their mansions and into the factories to do their part for the US of A."

2000

The Rosie the Riveter/WWII Home Front National Historical Park opens in Richmond, California, home of 55 war industries during WWII.

2002

Rockwell's *Rosie the Riveter* painting is put up for auction and sells for $4,959,500.00.

2009

At a Rosie the Riveter reunion 85-year-old Naomi Parker Fraley sees the same Naval Air Station picture that Doyle saw, but has proof that she is the girl in the picture.

2015

Communications professor James J. Kimball tracks Naomi Parker Fraley down and helps her get credit for being the photographed Rosie.

Glossary

Allies [AL-ahyz]—the 26 nations that fought against the alliance of Nazi Germany, Fascist Italy, and Japan in World War II

armaments [ARM-a-mehntz]—military weapons, bullets, and other equipment

aviation [AY-vee-ay-shun]—the industry that builds airplanes

circulation [SIR-cue-lay-shun]—the total number of people who subscribe to a magazine or newspaper

discrimination [DIS-crim-i-nay-shun]—unfair treatment because of race, gender, age, or other factor

economic [ECK-o-nom-ick]—having to do with a country's money and resources

feminist [FEHM-i-nist]—someone who believes women should have equal rights with men

Great Depression [GRATE de-PRES-shun]—a time of severe downturn in the U.S. economy; the Depression lasted from 1929 until 1939.

hijab [HE-zhab]—a veil or headscarf sometimes worn by Muslim women

icon [EYE-cahn]—a popular and well-known symbol recognized by many people

patriotism [PAY-tree-o-tizm]—having a strong attachment and faithfulness to one's country

propaganda [prop-ah-GAN-da]—information that takes a strong point of view in order to convince people to agree

recruit [ree-CRUTE]—to sign someone up for something

riveter [RIV-eh-ter]—an automatic tool for drilling nails, or rivets, into metal; the person who uses such a tool

Read More

Parsons, Martin. *Women in World War II*. The History Detective Investigates. New York: Hachette, 2017.

Sherman, Jill. *Role of Women in World War II*. Eye Witness to World War II. New York: Momentum Press, 2016.

World War II: The Definitive Visual History. Smithsonian. New York: DK Children, 2015.

Internet Sites

Use FactHound to find Internet sites related to this book.

Here's all you do:
Visit *www.facthound.com*

Just type in 9781515779353 and go.

Super-cool stuff! Check out projects, games and lots more at
www.capstonekids.com

Critical Thinking Questions

1. During the 1940s the American government used widespread advertising campaigns to attract women to war work. What were some of the ideas and images these ads used to persuade women? Why do you think the ads were effective?

2. How did taking over jobs that men had done help women gain more independence during the war years? What benefits did they get from working outside the home? How did these benefits and experiences lead to changes in later decades? (Or, how did these women's work experiences create the seeds of change for later generations of women?)

3. What were Jim Crow laws? How did the work done by women of color during the war help open the door for the Civil Rights movement?

Index